For Sarah

Presented to you on the eve of the 150th Anniversary of the arrival of East Indians in Trinidad.

With Warmest Best Wishes

Ron Ramdin

3 May 1995

Diaspora = not only to Westindies — also A
Malaya; & further east.

ABOUT RON RAMDIN

The historian and writer Ron Ramdin was born in Trinidad. (His grandfather who died in 1954 was an indentured labourer). He has lived and worked in England since 1962. After leaving drama school he obtained his BSc degree at the London School of Economics and Political Science. He studied Industrial Relations at the University of Middlesex and has had an active long-standing commitment to the trade union movement, being elected the first Staff Side Secretary of the Whitley Council when the British Library was formed in 1973.

Apart from his work as a free-lance journalist for the *BBC Caribbean Magazine*, Ron Ramdin has contributed many book reviews and articles to newspapers and journals. He has presented academic papers at an International Symposium of Caribbeanists, given the opening paper at the International Conference marking the 150th Anniversary of the arrival of East Indians in the Caribbean (University of Warwick) and at the Blacks in London Conference (University of London). He has also lectured internationally at the Sorbonne, France; at the University of Seville, Spain; at polytechnics, town halls, public libraries and schools in Britain, and has appeared on television and given radio interviews both in Britain and the Caribbean. In 1991 he presented the Tunde Jegede Ensemble and gave the Introduction at the inaugural performance of African Classical Music in Britain at the Purcell Room in London, and subsequently at Sadlers' Wells Theatre.

Ron Ramdin has written extensively. His books include *From Chattel Slave To Wage Earner, The Making of the Black Working Class In Britain*; *Paul Robeson: The Man And His Mission* and *The World In View: West Indies* - published both in Britain and the United States as a school text book. His new book *Arising From Bondage: A History of East Indians in the Caribbean 1838-1993* will be published in 1994. He is currently working on a biography of C.L.R. James and a book on Spain.

Ron Ramdin has received the prestigious Scarlet Ibis Award from the Trinidad and Tobago High Commission in London and the Hansib Community Award (1990) for outstanding and meritorious service towards a better understanding of racial issues in Britain.

PUBLISHER'S NOTE

Ron Ramdin first uncovered Captain Swinton's *Journal* 15 years ago. The publication of this facsimile now 135 years after it was first printed is invaluable and timely, given that, until very recently, few (if any) Caribbean scholars had actually seen it.

It is possible that only one other living historian (from Britain) has seen and used part of this material. Be that as it may, we are indebted to Ron Ramdin for retrieving this primary source material from obscurity and making it available not only for scholars and students, but also for the enlightenment of the general reading public.

The Other Middle Passage will complement the eleven titles already published in Hansib's *Coolie Odyssey* series, started in 1988 with *India in the Caribbean,* to commemorate the 150th anniversary of indentured labour in the Westindies* (1838-1988), and has since been a continuing process to fill a gap of much needed literature about Indian indentured immigrants and their descendents. Given that the majority population in Guyana are descendents of Indian indentured labourers, in Trinidad and Tobago they constitute approximately half the population and in Surinam over 40 per cent are "coolie" descendents, it is an aberration that people in authority, especially governing agencies have seen it fit to actively ignore the presence, culture and contributions of the Caribbean "coolie" at all levels of life.

I hope that a new democratic Guyana with a "coolie" President Dr.

* 'Westindies' (not 'West Indies') has been used in all Hansib publications since 1973 in a tribute to the formation of the Caribbean Community (CARICOM) at Chaguarmas, Trinidad, on 4 July 1973 and as an appropriation of the name given by the "discoverers" to assert the region's united, unique and distinctive identity.

Cheddi Jagan whose *Forbidden Freedom* is part of Hansib's *Coolie Odyssey* series, has the courage to ensure the appreciation of **all** cultures, so much ignored throughout the colonial and post-colonial history of his nation over the past 155 years.

Arif Ali
Hansib Publishing

INTRODUCTION

European economic expansion in the fifteenth century, generated great interest among enterprising explorers who sought a sea route to the riches of the East (to India and the land of the Great Khan). This quest which led Christopher Columbus to travel westward across the Atlantic Ocean, brought him instead to the islands of the Westindies on his first landfall in the New World. At that time, and even until his death he was convinced that his dream had become reality, that he had indeed reached the Indies and he called the natives Indians.

Soon after his arrival in the Westindies, the uncommonly ambitious and wealth-seeking explorer carried an item on his ships that would have profound implications, not only on the indigenous peoples (the Caribs and Arawaks), but also for generations yet unborn, from far-off lands, thus changing the course of European, African and Asian history.

He introduced the sugar cane plant on his second voyage to the Westindies, and thereafter the enforced labour endemic in the production of sugar for European consumption (which followed the search for gold) led to the destruction of the native Westindians, the first of the Caribbean peoples to resist their European oppressors. This decimation led, over a period of time, to a repeopling of the plantations first, by unsatisfactory White indentured labour, before African slaves were brought in to satisfy the insatiable European demand for sugar.

Consequently, African slavery and the slave trade reached new and barbaric heights, especially in the eighteenth century, when depravity was widespread in England, a time it was said, when the background of those who transported the slaves from Africa to the British colonies, was questionable. Generally, Englishmen adopted a swagger, and imbued with a buccaneering spirit, it seemed, they were "without shame of any sort", wrote one Englishman of a later age, "without in fact a single redeeming feature if we accept a certain bull dog tenacity when it came to a fight, and at times a reckless generosity in helping a friend. Every man was out to satisfy his own depraved lusts and cared not a curse whom they trampled in the dirt". The times were brutish and memorably evoked in the writings of Fielding and Smollett. This moral bankruptcy made rampant slavery less distasteful and unacceptable than it might have been, as slaves were openly sold in London and Liverpool. The attitude towards Blacks was clearly reflected in the fact that as the property of their masters, they had to be secured but in a way that was little removed from animals. In fact, the same manufacturers were used to make silver padlocks and collars for both dogs and Blacks! But, the English were not the only nation "deeply dyed in the blood of West Africa". So, too, were the Spanish, Portuguese, French and Dutch, as the slave trading monopoly ended and the "vile trade" was thrown open.

Merchants plied their trade, with the aim of making large profits from their ships' voyages during the "Middle Passage", from West Africa to the Caribbean and the Americas. In general, the attitude of the slave ships' captains towards their human cargoes were quite predictable. More humane captains, such as John Newton (who had earlier in his slaving career seen and experienced the depths of human misery and despair) and Crow (a man who after having doubts about the slave trade, embraced it and became a legendary figure), were nevertheless few and far between. But in this risky "business of blood", the goal was to land as many African slaves alive as possible. Inhibiting and frustrating the achievement of this were the design and capacity of the ships, which were used to transport the Africans. Around 1760, the British slave ships known as "Guineamen" weighed about 200 tons; and 16 years later a "typical slaver" such as the *Brooks* had a tonnage of 297 tons. On her 1786 voyage she carried 609 slaves, though only licensed for four hundred and fifty. The lack of space continued to be the bane of the Africans who were transported across the Atlantic.

The horrors of the "Middle Passage" (from Africa to the Westindies and the Americas) though often mentioned in relation to the African Slave Trade and slavery is rarely described. The involuntary entry of the slaves into the slave ships and their journey across the high seas was a nightmare that few (if any) would willingly endure. One writer has noted that there were "instances of ships losing 50 of their slaves in the passage through the tropics", not to mention the other tragedies at sea, arising from the profit motive. Suffering was endemic:

> "The men suffered the most for they were chained leg to leg and hand to hand, so that it was impossible for them to shift their cramped position. The Rev. John Newton, (who later wrote the hymn "Amazing Grace"), the reformed Guinea Captain declared that he had often seen a living man chained to a dead man. The slave irons took up room, and sometimes, in a very crowded ship, all the men could not be ironed, so the weakly and sick were left free of shackles; this allowed them to be packed like sardines, in layers, one on top of the other, so that *each living man had less room than a dead man in his coffin;* and if they did not crowd up close enough, they were lashed with cat-o-nine tails, the ever-ready weapon of the slaver".

Through trial and error, the capacity and improvements of the ships, benefited the investors who profited hugely at the expense of the captive Africans. Once the Slave Trade and African slavery were abolished and the Apprenticeship system ended, various short-lived, unsuccessful labour experiments, (which included Portuguese and Chinese labour) were put into operation in the British colonies. Drawing upon the labour resources of the East remained a possibility, moreso from India than elsewhere. Eventually, the introduction of East Indian indentured labourers, effectively filled the colonial plantations' labour vacuum.

The *Avon* (1,572 tons) in Calcutta.
Built in 1884, it was one of the James Nourse fleet of "Coolie Ships"

The "Coolie Ships"

No sooner had slavery been abolished, and indeed while Apprenticeship was still in effect, the idea (given the problems endemic in the long sea journey) of introducing "Coolie* labour" from India to the Caribbean was finally translated into action.

And so, in 1838, while slavers and cruisers were still employed on the high seas, "Coolie ships" were engaged in the trade of carrying indentured Indians from far beyond the eastern shores of the Atlantic. The arrival of the *Whitby* and *Hesperus* (the latter 330 tons and carrying 249 emigrants) in Guyana in 1838, heralded a new enterprise and a new traffic via the other "Middle Passage". Thus began the final phase of the last mass influx of cheap, and strictly controlled plantation labour to the Caribbean, through the institution of the East Indian indentureship system and East Indian emigration which fed it. (Stops and starts there were: for example, East Indian emigration was stopped in 1839 - resumed in 1845; stopped again in 1848 - resumed in 1851, and continued until the indentured labour system ended in 1917).

Trinidad received its first shipment of indentured Indians when the *Fatel Rozack* arrived on 30th May 1845. In the succeeding twelve years, no fewer than a dozen ships had brought thousands more to the island. By then, it had already become clear that both the "Coolie ships" and the long voyages to the Caribbean were fraught with dangers. The hazardous journey was particularly so during the 1850s. In spite of the first set of rules for Indian emigration being implemented in 1845, (recognition of the unacceptable, cramped passenger space on the ships and the 1855 *Instructions to Surgeons of Vessels* conveying Indians from the Westindies to India) for hundreds of Indian emigrants (including those on the ill-fated *Shah Allum*** bound for Mauritius in 1859)

* The word "coolie" was used by the end of the eighteenth century to describe labourers at the bottom of the industrial market. ** In the opinion of historian Hugh Tinker, as stated in *A New System of Slavery* (Hansib Publishing), the identity of the ship in relation to this famous tragedy is "curiously blurred". He argued that it was not the *Shah Jehan*, (which was recorded in the *Mauritius Report on Immigration* of 1865 as still being in service!) but the *Shah Allur* which had lost all 399 Indians.

travelling in the 1850s to the Westindies, the much needed reforms came too late. Nevertheless, by comparison with the African slavers, following abolition of the British slave trade and slavery, humanitarian concern and the reluctance of some officials to engage in a new system of slavery, resulted in the more spacious "Coolie ships".

Let us briefly consider the main factors involved in the drama of this traffic: who owned the "Coolie ships" and how they were administered and run.

The leading companies operating a service in this passage were Sandbach, Tinne and Company; and James Nourse, both of whom were preceded by Gillanders, Arbuthnot and Company. Moreover, there were a few ships known as "Outsiders", which occasionally carried Indians to Trinidad and Guyana. (The ships of John Allan were essentially concerned with the carriage of indentured emigrants to Mauritius).

Taken together, these companies (especially Sandbach Tinne and Company) provided a service from as early as 1828.

In general, the construction of this type of ship was such that the emigrants were allocated as follows: married couples occupied the middle section, single women the rear end, while single men, (usually the largest group) where at the forward section.

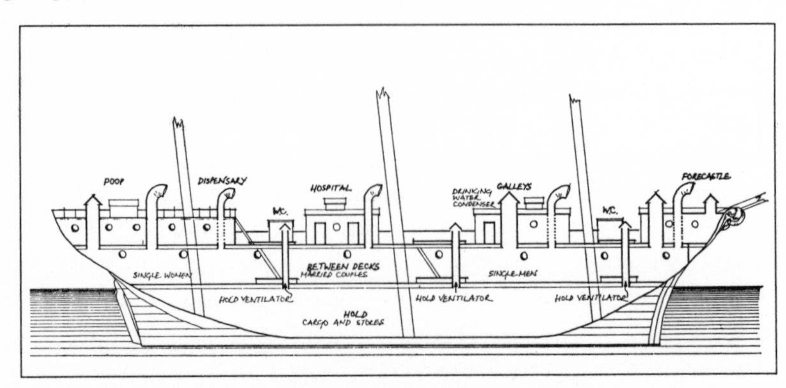

Cross-section of a "coolie ship"*c.* 1880
Courtesy Hugh Tinker - *A New System of Slavery*(Hansib Publishing)

G. R Sandbach

J. E. Tinne

The ships that travelled to Trinidad and Guyana (and Mauritius) were strictly regulated by Emigration Acts of both the British and Westindian Governments, to ensure that adequate attention was given to the Indians aboard.

Apart from the Captain, who determined the course of the voyage, the "Coolie" ships' staff hierarchy (especially in the later stages of this traffic) included the Surgeon-Superintendent, Third Officer, Third Mate and Engineer, (Chief Officer), Compounders, Sirdars, Bandharries and Topazes.

The Surgeon-Superintendent of an Indian "Coolie ship", at least by the 1850s, was regarded as being in many respects equal, if not more important, than the Captain. He was directly answerable to the government official known as the Protector of Immigrants, who had appointed him. His duties included inspection not only of the Indians, selecting the fit from the unfit, but also of the ship followed by a report on ventilation, cooking arrangements, the deck-house hospital and the ships' provisions.

Surgeons of emigrant ships adhered to the Trinidad Government

Instructions, which required such persons to monitor the Captain and the officers of the ship in their relations with the emigrants. His relations with the ship's officers, he was cautioned, required the exercise of at least some degree of discretion and firmness, which he was expected to apply in his dealings with the indentured emigrants. The exercise of these qualities, he was reminded, depended "not less on your own comfort than the success of the voyage".

The Surgeon-Superintendent's power and responsibility on these ships was undoubted. Much depended upon him. "Cut off for weeks and even months from the outside world", noted one historian, "the lives of Indians were in the hands of the Surgeon whose personal resourcefulness or incompetence could never really be known until he had faced and overcome an emergency".

Indian and Eurasian doctors from the Calcutta Medical School, were employed on the shorter voyages to Mauritius and Malaya. But, it took repeated tragedy on the long haul of the Westindian voyages, before the Emigration Commissioners and colonial agents bothered to employ experienced British doctors. By its very nature, the job of the "Coolie", ship's doctor was far from being adventurous. Indeed, it was largely lonely, and monotonous, though at times it could be very demanding. If the clever and ambitious were less likely to be recruited, what kind of men were actually drawn to this post? Two kinds were identified: first the sort of person who was a loner and with an unconventional approach to life; and second, the adherent of authority and paternalism, attracted by the big challenge and heavy responsibility. The latter type was, of course, to be found in key positions throughout the British Empire.

The crucial issue of pay was dependent upon the health of the Indians on board the ships. A pay review of the Surgeon-Superintendent on such ships, conducted by the Emigration Commissioners in London in May 1857, increased the eight shillings received for every Indian landed alive, to ten shillings for each person on the first voyage, eleven shillings on the second voyage, and twelve shillings on subsequent voyages. The doctors faced the dilemma of how best to keep the Indians alive. In his

The *Forth*, a James Nourse ship of 1820 tons, built in 1894

frustration, John Bury, a Surgeon-Superintendent wrote from Trinidad on 25 March 1857 of the Indians committed to his care "whose habits and language he is in most cases ignorant and who, unfortunately, are peculiarly susceptible of... cholera and dysentery: one, if not both of which invariably make their appearance in a few hours after leaving port, and who can tell when or where their fearful ravages may stop? When stricken by one serious malady they quickly lie down to die, seldom making application for them... In many cases he has to inflict some punishment before he can get them to take food or medicine. Many of their habits, too, are most disgusting... I have no hesitation in saying that his duties are five times as heavy as on board an English Emigrant vessel." Was this doctor's motive humanitarian or purely economic?

The Surgeon-Superintendents of Indian emigrant ships, especially in the early days, not only sought men who were "rough", but also those who, by 1860, were generally untrustworthy. In the wake of the exceptionally high mortality on voyages to the Westindies during the years 1856 to 1869, in spite of a reduction, the Emigration Commissioners still expressed concern. Dr. S. B. Partridge, writing as Medical Inspector of emigrants at Calcutta in September 1865 was of the view that professional men with exceptional talent and education were unlikely to seek employment in the emigration service; and seven years later, this was endorsed by Dr. Grant.

But even though there were a number of unsatisfactory Surgeon-Superintendents on the "Coolie ships", in the decade that followed, many doctors had indeed showed competence.

Although the Surgeon's relations with the Captain of the ship was often uneasy, his fundamental charge was to ensure that as many of the indentured Indians as possible reached their destinations alive. The pay ("head money") he received, therefore, depended on the Indians' survival during the journey. While the Surgeon received ten shillings for each indentured Indian landed alive, a fee which tended to rise to 21 shillings (at least in the early days of the "Coolie trade"), an unsatisfactory shipment resulted in forfeiture. "It was very necessary that the Surgeon-Superintendent, should be up to his work on the Indian coolie ships", wrote Lubbock, "for the Indians, unlike the Chinese who is very hard to kill, had many ways of dying during the voyage". The Indians, he said, (making his point perhaps too simplistically) were prone to jump overboard, to commit suicide if roughly spoken to or falsely accused of something. Cholera, however, remained the terror of the "Coolie trade", especially in the early years of the traffic when the medical inspection prior to embarkation from India was less strict than it became later.

For all their trustworthiness, Surgeon-Superintendents have been known to be very unpopular, as was the case when Indian emigrants rose in revolt against the occupant of this post on the *Hesperides*. Furthermore, Surgeon-Superintendents were, more often than not, neither liked by the Captain nor the ship's officers.

Excluded from deck work, the Third Mate of the emigrant ships, performed the duties of Purser, taking charge of the emigrants stores. He worked closely with the Surgeon, whose endorsement was necessary before his work as Third Mate could be paid at the rate of 2s. 6d. for every Indian indentured labourer that disembarked. Given that an Indian emigrant ship often made four trips in a period ranging from 14 to 18 months (for example, between Guyana - Calcutta - Fiji; Fiji - Calcutta; and Calcutta - Trinidad) with 500 to 800 Indians, the Third Mate's earnings for this period ranged from £300 - £400. Though he received his orders from the Surgeon-Superintendent, having charge of the ship's stores, he was often the captain's cohort.

Also working directly under the charge of the Surgeon- Superintendent was the ship's Engineer, who was responsible for condensing the water and providing the steam for cooking. Of necessity, he rose early in the morning, to ensure that the fire in the furnace would be ready by about 5.30 am so that preparation of the Indians' breakfast consisting of "kitcherries", (which required two to two and a half hours boiling) could begin. He was expected to condense an estimated 800 gallons of water, which means the condenser was almost in constant use. Not surprisingly, one of the identifying characteristics of a "coolie ship" at sea, was, as one writer put it, "her very black mainsail, caused by the smoke from the donkey boiler of the condenser".

Next in line of those who worked on the ship, were the Compounders, ("baboos" as they were referred to) who played the important role of mediating between the emigrants and the Surgeon-Superintendent.

Described as Indian petty officers under the direction of the Surgeon, the Sirdars, who assisted in keeping discipline among their fellow-Indians, also helped in the distribution of rations and took charge of the preparation of food. There was a ratio of five Sirdars (including a Head Sirdar) to every 100 emigrants. Their appointment by the Emigration Agent at the Depot was subject to change, depending on their conduct which was appraised by the Surgeon-Superintendent.

The Bandharries, largely drawn from the higher castes and employed at the Emigration Depot, were also the responsibility of the Surgeon. This category of the ships' staff were immediately supervised by a Head Bandharry.

"Coolie" sweepers aboard *Avoca*, a James Nourse "Coolie ship" of 1703 tons, built in 1885

Indian 'Lascar' crew of the*Avoca*

Unlike the Bandharries, the Topazes were men of low caste. Known as "sweepers" in India, we are told that they were relatively "well paid" for their menial cleaning tasks. How ironic that these traditionally "unclean" men were to be seen constantly cleaning - washing, drying and sweeping, not only the "coolies" quarters, but also the main decks!

It is clear then, that the lower levels of the ships' administration was designed to ensure the best possible treatment of the Indians, so that the gain, in terms of the pay of all concerned with a given voyage, could be maximized.

The two main Emigration Depots were at Calcutta and Madras, the ports of embarkation for the ships that made their way often with difficulty through the Bay of Bengal and past Sri Lanka (fomerly Ceylon), down the Indian Ocean, along the Mozambique channel, round the Cape of Good Hope, then up the Atlantic and past the island of St. Helena, before proceeding to the Caribbean.

By 1858 (some twenty years after the *Whitby* and *Hesperus* had arrived in Guyana and thirteen years after the *Fatel Rozack* had brought its first group of Indian indentured labourers to Trinidad) no fewer than thirteen emigrant ships had completed the voyage from India to Port of Spain, Trinidad. Hitherto, shipwrecks and disasters at sea there were, in the course of the "coolie" traffic, but few, have been so haunted by insistent destruction as the daily terror that assailed the *Salsette* and the Indians on board for the duration of their long voyage from Calcutta to Trinidad in 1858. As it happened, the ship's Captain Edolphus Swinton (whether or not he was in the habit of keeping a diary) decided, on this occasion, to write down his day to day thoughts, as he commandeered his vessel (no doubt, with the safety of his passengers in his mind) on the high seas, between the lands of the Far East and the West. Did his earlier doubts of the emigrants' poor condition at the Immigration Depot in India prompt this action? Be that as it may, in retrospect, the Captain's greatest service to the Indian emigrants, ("Coolies" as they were disparagingly referred to in the official literature of the time), was the act of recording for posterity his account of the voyage; a very rare and invaluable historical document. All the more so, because it is one of only two known *first-hand* accounts that have survived voyages of Indian emigrant ships bound for Trinidad, and the *only* known Captain's "Diary" (The other is the account of the *Delharee* in 1859, by the ship's doctor.) By comparison, what was significant about Captain Swinton's *Journal* (and the investigation that followed upon his request) is the light it sheds on a number of related aspects of East Indian indentured emigration to the Caribbean.

With Captain Swinton in command and Dr. John Dyer as Surgeon-Superintendent, the *Salsette* (579 tons, built in Sunderland, England in 1854, with its home port of Newcastle was owned by Mr. E. Mounsy) left Calcutta on 17 March 1858, with 324 Indian emigrants, most of whom were people from the hilly areas of Chota Nagpur, known as "Junglees". Captain Swinton had experienced tragedy the year before, while transporting Chinese "Coolies" from Hong Kong to Australia, and was well placed to observe the Indians as they were preparing to embark on the *Salsette*. Both he and Dr. Dyer were unhesitant making, as it turned out, prescient comments relating to the generally unsatisfactory physical appearance of the emigrants. But they were over-ruled, their views ignored, as the urgent need to fill the ship, it seemed, took precedence over obvious medical considerations. In fact, it became clear later that the depot's medical inspector was inexperienced in attending to Indians on board emigrant ships.

As was the case in the African slave trade, the "Coolie ships" also had a number of notorious captains. Increasingly, however, this was counter-balanced by the appointment of less severe men, even though they were no less self-seeking. The "Extracts" from the diary of Captain Swinton was published in London in February 1859 by Alfred W. Bennett, at the price of sixpence. If writing the *Journal* was an initial act of good faith (and by implication, for historians, one of good fortune), then its presentation to his wife for safe-keeping was another act of

Indian children at breakfast on a "Coolie ship".
Many children and infants perished on the voyage of the*Salsette* in 1858.

special merit in what was otherwise a sequence of tragic events on this incredible voyage. Another seemingly strange coincidence is the fact that it was unusual for wives to accompany their husbands, on such ventures involving "Coolie emigrants". So why was she on this voyage? And if she had not been on this journey would the Captain's *Journal* have survived? James Carlisle, Minister of Salem Chapel in Woolwich, London, who edited the *Journal,* respectfully dedicated it to the philanthropic Society of Friends, with whom he had been associated all his public life. He informs us in his editorial note that within a few days of leaving Trinidad, Captain Swinton and his crew had drowned in the Atlantic, and saddened by his death, his widow transcribed the extracts of the diary into what became the published*Journal*. As Editor, Carlisle and the Society of Friends vouched for the "accuracy of the copy", and prefaces the *Journal* with his own comments on the excessive mortality, all the more puzzling because there was "no kind of epidemic" among the Indians. He posed the questions that many would ask later: "How shall we account for such mortality - an average of more than one per day during the entire passage?" he wrote. "Was the captain at fault? a thoughtless, bold, dashing sailor, reckless of human life?" No, Carlisle, replied. In fact, the Captain was "kind, generous and humane", foregoing the luxuries of his position and actively tended to the pitiful "dying coolies" with his wife, of whom Carlisle wrote: "she was like another Florence Nightingale in the hospital at Scutari; but for the attendance and care of this angel of mercy, humanly speaking the mortality, large as it was, would have been much larger". So, out of this tragedy, a heroine had emerged.

The published version of the *Journal* (for which Captain Swinton will be remembered) did not contain entries for each day of the voyage, which lasted from 17 March to 2 July. Within the first four entries, however, he mentioned three deadly afflictions of the emigrants - cholera, dysentery and diarrhoea; and deaths from not eating. The psychological effects arising from the cramped conditions at the depot, separation from their families and loved ones, and the element of uncertainty that troubled

The "Coolie ship" *Erne* (1692 tons), in background at St. Helena owned by James Nourse, was built in 1886.

them, were not hitherto seriously considered. By the 28 March, eleven days out, infants were dying "for want of milk" and adults were denied food to their liking, such as dried fish. Among the first to suspect a tragic situation developing was the Captain's wife Jane, who helped to feed the sick with arrowroot and sago. But so early in the journey, not even the Topaze could interpret the cause of certain deaths when approached by the ship's doctor. On this journey, there was some evidence (or suspicion that emigrants who had earlier been rejected, were now allowed to enter the ship, because those emigrating wanted to stay as a family unit. And, as the days passed, it became clear that some emigrants who were "too old", tended to die of a combination of old age, diarrhoea and debility. But not all of the 124 emigrants who had died, were old and /or infirm. Many infants, young boys and girls and young men and women had passed away with surprising suddenness.

Fear was ever-present among the emigrants, and doubtful of their destination, Captain Swinton now reflected on the observation that the Indians tended to "pine after being put on board". He was concerned about separating the sick from those who were well and cleared the launch boat, which was converted into a hospital. But the smell of sickness and death was so overwhelming, in spite of everything having been done to prevent it. He regretted not having done this on leaving Calcutta, and believed that the lives of many Indians would have been saved, because their sickness arose "entirely from bad smells". He administered hot baths to children, and was wary of the cold weather which deterred him "from turning the boat into a hospital", even though as time would prove, this was a necessity. But his thorough cleansing and purification of the ship was not as effective as he had hoped.

Forty days into the voyage (which lasted 108 days) dysentery, diarrhoea and cholera were taking a firmer hold of its victims on a regular basis each day. The Indians were weak and could not or did not eat the food presented to them. To stop the general debility and deaths, the captain and his wife paid very close attention to the unfolding horror on their lonely ship. Still the Indians died. "A great reformation", Captain Swinton wrote "is required in the system of Cooley emigration". The doctor wanted medicine ("chalk mixture") and asked the Captain if the *Salsette* would be calling at the island of St. Helena, where he hoped to replenish his supply of chalk powder and laudanum (opium), which were vital in his medical ministrations of the Indians. The Captain's response to the doctor was "not unless he insisted on it", because he explained, "it would put the ship to considerable expense by doing so". The unacceptable circumstances clearly demanded urgent action which had yet to be taken. Within a few days, more Indians died and the doctor's patience, having reached its limit, now forced him to beg the Captain to stop at St. Helena for the necessary medicines. The Captain did so. But we must note that he agreed to this *not* for humanitarian reasons, but "in compliance with the terms of the charter party".

The stop at St. Helena did not stem the incessant mournful sounds, the whimpers, the moans, the cries for help and the daily deaths, while the ship rocked to and fro, as it made its way northwestwards over the changeable, glassy surface of the Atlantic waters. The ship was on the last leg of the journey and the Captain kept in close contact with his Indian interpreters, one of whom had tallied that by the 6th June, 105 Indians had succumbed to death. Although this figure was unusually high, the Captain, seemingly lacking confidence in his Interpreters, nevertheless tended to rely on the information he received from them.

Dysentery, diarrhoea and cholera remained the scourge of the ship, and on 30th June, Captain Swinton made his own count to find that of the 324 emigrants who had embarked at Calcutta, only 108 men, 61 women, 30 children under the age of ten, two infants and two interpreters were left. At this stage, he feared that three more would die before they reached Port of Spain. When the voyage, lasting more than three months was over, and the *Salsette* had finally entered the safe haven of Trinidad waters, the creaking, weather-beaten vessel was boarded on 2 July (a girl of 15 had died that day) by Dr. Anderson, the Trinidad Harbour Master. Predictably, after such an ordeal, the Indians would have looked awful. Not surprisingly, therefore, this official had no doubt that the "Coolies" were "a miserable set", and described the mortality of 124 deaths, as "dreadful". Even though they were safe now from the battering force of the sea, high and low temperatures, high winds and heavy rains, for some (much too young or too ill to understand or care) the situation was none the less hopeless. The next day, a three-year old girl died and Dr. Mitchell, the Agent-General of Immigrants (or Protector) inspected the 199 Indians still alive (of "tolerably good condition") and 12 of them (five men, six women and one boy) were sent to the Colonial Hospital. Five others (one man, one boy and three girls - orphans) were taken to the Indians Training School and Orphan Asylum at Tacarigua. Officially, reference to "man" was the term used in the reckoning up of "passage money" - 10 years of age being considered an adult. Henry Mitchell wrote, on 10th July, to the Colonial Secretary stating that he

The *Ganges II* (1529 tons), another of the James Nourse "Coolie ships" built in 1882

proposed to offer his comments on the "casualties attending the present system of Indian immigration to Trinidad", once he had an opportunity of examining the report and journal of Dr. John Dyer, the Surgeon-Superintendent of the *Salsette*.

Writing from Port of Spain to the Colonial Secretary on 3 July, Dr. Anderson (Inspector of Health of Shipping) after conferring with Dr. Dyer and the Topazes, expressed his informed view of the causes of the deaths thus:

"It results that many of these people were Sangalee, that is to say, inhabiting swampy jungle, and were sent on board with sickly constitutions, rendering them more susceptible of disease. Concurrent causes were also to be found in this having been the last ship, and freighted with subjects rejected by those which hadsailed before. Also, the obnoxious biscuit diet, which the medical men of other immigrant ships have condemned as unfitted to the Hindoo constitution, was given every other day and the dhal was of an inferior quality. The accommodation and ventilation" (this contradicts the Captain's entry on the 2 July, when he stated that Dr. Anderson and other harbour officials were "well-pleased" with the ventilation and accommodation) "are moreover not so good as usually found in East India ships, and there was a noisome smell between decks. As might be expected, the physical appearance of these coolies was below average, and they have as a whole a sickly and defected look; twelve are reported to be sent to hospital, one of whom appeared to be in a dying state.

"Superadded to these reasons, these people are dirty and to my inquiries on this subject, the answer was that the only clothing they had was that on their bodies, and no change had been provided for them".

And much too late, Dr. Mitchell added his "disapprobation of the Calcutta emigration management", as the sick Indians were taken away to the local hospital.

To his disappointment, when Captain Swinton arrived at last on Trinidad soil and had spoken to Dr. Mitchell, he found that only 182 adults had landed alive! Disturbed by the number of deaths, and mindful of his agent's warning before he had left Calcutta (which meant a cut in salary), he requested an investigation which was granted.

Before the report was completed, from his Immigration Office, Henry Mitchell stated his view of Dr. Dyer's suitability as the prospective Surgeon-Superintendent, should the *Salsette* undertake a shipment of returned Indians. "I am not of opinion", he said, "That the mortality among the coolies under his charge in the *Salsette* was attributable in any way to deficient skill or attention on his part".

When Mitchell finally submitted his report to the Governor on 23 July 1868, he opened by saying that "the diarrhoea and dysentery, which caused serious mortality on board the *Salsette* and other vessels, long after the deaths from cholera had ceased, do not appear to have been attributable to any single source."

He commented on the *Salsette's* capacity and readiness for emigration purposes, citing its prior voyage, carrying 500 Chinese emigrants from Hong Kong to Australia, with little loss of life, and Dr. Dyer's proven expertise as a doctor. He then addressed the question of ventilation and the provision of stern ports on the ship, and he regretted the "counteracting influences" which wreaked havoc on the ship, feeling that but for this, a "satisfactory state of health" among the Indian emigrants could have been reasonably assured and result in low mortality. As it was, from the first day to the last, the spectre of death haunted the ship. He emphasized his "careful and repeated examination" of the ship, her officers and the Surgeon-Superintendent and his journals, which led to the conclusion that however "complex" were the sources of this unusual number of deaths, they could not be attributed "to deficient care or skill in the parties" who administered to the desperate malaise of the Indians during the voyage. Mitchell then went on to enumerate the causes, as he saw them, that were the "most likely to have contributed directly or indirectly" to the deaths of the Indian emigrants, who had braved the high seas in the last two seasons. First, he identified that of the 124 Indians who had died, 120 were "Junglie coolies" or "lower Bengalees", people who were not of "vigorous frame". In time, these "Junglies", he said, became the "most docile and the most laborious race", once they had landed safely in Trinidad. In fact, this was also said of them, at the time of their introduction to the Caribbean, during the "Gladstone experiment" in Guyana.

But, he observed that for a considerable time, they remained in a depressed state, the effects of death and despondency endemic in their unforgettable experience of seasickness. Secondly, in this state, the biscuit diet and the change from "light" meals to a "more generous allowance" aggravated their sickly condition. Thirdly, the Indian emigrants' neglect in informing the doctor of the early symptoms of diarrhoea or dysentery, was likely to lead to cholera and death. Furthermore, Mitchell argued, drugs alone was insufficient, and stressed the importance of "words of consolation" in the Indians' native tongue which were more than likely to bring them to life. Fourthly, as Immigration Agent, he recommended that the space-consuming bed fittings should be replaced by "boards of a proper dimension"; and finally, that while the deficient ventilation had not been one of the main causes of sickness, it should not be overlooked. He therefore suggested that in future sick emigrants should receive attention in a hospital provided on the ship's deck, which would have the beneficial effect of keeping apart the sick from the healthy, thus helping to "save the majority of the immigrants from the sight of sickness and suffering, an influence which is in itself always lowering".

Moreover, at this stage of East Indian emigration to the Caribbean, Mitchell called for a better quality of emigrants, and improved housing and general conditions at the emigration depot, until the emigrants had grown used to the diet on board ship. He recommended that biscuit should *not* be given to the emigrants unless stated as their preference; that the medical attendant should not only speak the Indians' language, but should also have the assistance of two native Indians "to relieve him from menial duties". He reiterated the importance of altering certain fittings on ships, the provision of woollen clothing during the periods of cold weather (especially around the Cape), and emphasized the provision of a hospital on the ship's deck. This last point was suggested by Dr. Dyer, Surgeon-Superintendent of the *Salsette*, with whom Henry Mitchell agreed.

Attached to Mitchell's report, was a copy of Dr. Dyer's observations on the high mortality of the emigrants under his charge. He confirmed the problems of the "Junglies" (Lower Bengalies), constituting over two-thirds of the Indians on the *Salsette* who, in his estimation were "far more prone to disease and far less amenable to treatment than the Upper Bengalies or townspeople". He could not distinguish between these two classes, before the voyage of the *Salsette*, and *en route*, had eventually to rely upon the Topazes to point out individuals from these groups. The difference of relative mortality was "startling": of the 101 Upper Bengalies, four had died (or four per cent), whilst of the 223 Lower Bengalies, 120 had died (or 53.8 per cent). From these figures, Dyer deduced that the Junglies "seem to be a weaker and more dirty race than the others; they are more lazy in their habits, and there is far more difficulty in enforcing cleanliness among them". He observed a tendency among the Indians to discard their "foul clothes" over the ship's side, rather than wash them, so that by the time that the*Salsette* arrived at the Cape, many of the emigrants were "almost without any clothing". The children (among whom the mortality was greatest) suffered most from this want of clothing, and to meet the urgent need, Dyer tells us that he took "the precaution of having the clothes of those who died... well washed... and put by," so that he could distribute them to the sick and half-naked Indians during the inclement weather of the Cape.

Dyer felt justified in concluding that the Junglies were by far, the least fitted for the very long voyage from India to the Caribbean, and that their reluctance to accept, indeed resistance to medical treatment, compounded their weakened condition. Therefore, he felt it might be worthwhile to recruit a "Jungly (Bengalie) practitioner... to assist the Surgeon-Superintendent". He criticised the Junglies for their "idle" and "lazy" habits, which frustrated his best efforts to arouse their interest in taking exercise. Not until a week after they had left St. Helena, did he have "any measure of success" and this was achieved by enforcing a daily regime of exercise. He then addressed the question of the biscuit diet, which was disagreeable to the Junglies, causing their bowel complaint. But if this was so, why did such a diet continue for the duration of that long journey? Dyer felt bound to state: "in justice to myself, I must add that it had not been mentioned to me previous to our arrival here, although I have often questioned the Topazes concerning any food disagreeing with the Coolies". Given that a third of those who had died were infants or children, there was a desperate need for preserved milk; and the neglect of parents, death or separation from their parents, caused the children to pine, and many of them were found to be "greatly dejected in spirits", thus further exposing them to disease. Finally, in his "Memoranda", Dr. Dyer summarised the points he had made earlier, including the recruitment of more Topazes, one of whom "should be especially adapted as a nurse; good and assiduous nursing being more calculated to benefit those coolies when sick than any medical attendance or medicine"; and a separate hospital on deck.

The loss of life on this voyage (the worst on any "Coolie ship" except those that were wrecked) also resulted in more evidence, from Captain Swinton (in addition to his *Journal*) in which he spoke of the "very emaciated" look of the "miserable set" of Indians who had boarded the ship at Calcutta. Mr Caird, the Immigration Agent at Calcutta, contradicted this view. They were "as fine a set of people", he said, as he had seen shipped that season. Even though he was master of the ship, Swinton had to comply (against his better judgement) with the wishes of the Calcutta officials, taking on board biscuit, rice, dhal and pepper (in accordance with Government regulations) for the Indians. "They had biscuit every other day for breakfast", said Captain Swinton. "I cannot say that we ever suspected the biscuit was unwholesome". He pinpointed "crossing the line" of the southern latitudes as the time of greatest mortality on the *Salsette* and recalled that the weather was "very wet, for three or four days in succession", the cold weather off the Cape, lasting a fortnight. In these conditions, he said, he and others were as vigilant as they could possibly have been.

Three weeks after the ship had reached Trinidad, the Surgeon-Superintendent, Dr. Dyer recorded his considered comments on the Indian emigrants on the *Salsette*. Until the day before they had boarded, Dr. Dyer said he had never seen any "coolies" except those who had returned from Guyana. He had inspected the *Salsette's* emigrants with Dr. Scriven, a fellow-pupil at the Royal College of Surgeons in London, at the Bhowampore Depot, all in one day! While Dr. Dyer and Dr. Scriven were agreed that nine of the Indians should not go, the latter argued that they should all go, because there were "special reasons, such as having families on board". Dr. Scriven had his say, and the voyage went ahead. With hindsight, Dr. Dyer said he believed that the *Salsette* was filled with "the last people" at the depot; and that their medical examination seemed to have been rushed, taking just the one day. Dr. Dyer said he expressed his reservations of the Indians at the time, and begged Dr Scriven to "aid him in the best way he could". Of the Indians who were eventually shipped Dr. Dyer said "scarcely a dozen" could compete in terms of physical condition with people who came back from Guyana.

Outstanding defects demanded urgent attention and, it came as no surprise that in conclusion, he recommended the "substitution of blue shirts, or flannel or woollen wrapper... that in all the immigration vessels the hospital ought to be removed to the main deck" and that there ought to be a better class of assistants for the Surgeons on the ships. Other members of the *Salsette's* crew gave evidence, including John Passmore - Third Officer, and Peter Handyside - Chief Officer. In general, these officers confirmed the poor and sickly condition of the Indians who were on the *Salsette*.

Adding to the daily entries, in the published version of Captain Swinton's diary, his wife Jane recorded her cogent remarks. After all, she was there and had seen it all, a witness to each terrible day of the voyage. The Captain of an emigrant ship, she pointed out, had no voice either in the selection of the Indian emigrants or in the crucial choice of the doctor. His primary concern was to navigate the ship in accordance with the rules of the charter party. She was of the opinion that "the captain ought to be allowed to nominate a doctor on behalf of the owners, to make the selection of the coolies in conjunction with the doctor appointed to the ship, and that sufficient time be given to the doctors to make the proper inspection"; that the doctors should speak the Indians' language, "instead of being wholly dependent on an interpreter, who may understand English very differently".

Jane Swinton also addressed the manner of recruitment of the Indians in the countryside - inducement to emigrate with "fine promises", and suggested a period of one month at the depot, to ensure that the emigrants were in a fit state to undertake a three-month voyage. Referring to the Captain's diary, she said she did not believe that more than five of the emigrants either knew their destination or the kind of work they were expected to do. "My heart often yearned over them", she wrote, in

The *Avoca* on its way

Captain N. G. Hatch, Dr. Welsh and leading hands of the "coolie" emigrants aboard *Avoca*

thinking of the way they were entrapped, adding for good measure that a "great many on board were not calculated for the labour they would have to perform".

She suggested, *inter alia*, a diet better-suited to the Indians; that tank water should be substituted for Hooghly River water; and that well-selected female nurses be recruited. She endorsed the repeated recommendations of the above-mentioned officers - the necessity of a hospital on the deck of "coolie ships". She had no doubt that were it not for the unremitting attention of her husband and herself, the mortality would have been greater. "Why have one law for our Indian emigrants to the Westindian colonies, and another for our English emigrants to Australia?" she asked. This injustice towards Indian emigrants was a matter which Captain Swinton himself had hoped to put before the British Government, had he lived. "I hope that the few remarks which I have penned may", she wrote, "with the assistance of God, tend towards promoting the welfare of this unfortunate race of people, and may be a means of interesting some kind of philanthropic persons on their behalf. My heart sickens when I think of their sufferings; so I must conclude".

No one would deny the devoted attention that Captain and Mrs. Swinton paid to the Indians, to keep them alive. But while Mrs. Swinton veered towards a more humanitarian approach (expressing her concern also for the Chinese "coolie" traffic), the Captain was more concerned with the economic considerations of landing as many Indians alive as possible. Only the year before, the Indian Mutiny had aroused bitter feelings in Britain towards the "heathen Hindoos," and like the African slaves (who were still being transported to the Caribbean, while the "Coolie trade" was in progress) the Indian emigrants were primarily economic units. "The pecuniary interests of the ship's owners were at stake", Carlisle reminded us. "Every death that took place among the Coolies was to them a loss of thirteen pounds, so that by the deaths that did take place, they lost about £1500 of their charter money". In fact, Captain Swinton was sharply reminded of this by his Agent before the *Salsette* left Calcutta.

On the face of it, there seemed to have been much official concern about the sad voyage of the *Salsette*, yet little has been said about the Indians' sheer desperation, of the unrealistic hopes they had harboured which helped them to transcend the stultifying effects of their wretched lives and, indeed, having made the courageous decision and then taking the first steps on an unimaginably hazardous journey; and significantly, one that had the added dimension (at least, for the Hindus among them) of caste pollution, which further tested their resolve. Throughout this traffic, Officialdom remained largely unmoved, except by their own nineteenth century authoritarian preoccupations. And to expect more from a privileged and foreign elite was perhaps expecting too much. Whether or not the Indians were of "inferior" quality as potential labourers, it is clear that they were *all*(regardless of caste, class, colour or religion), perceived by European administrators, as being of an inferior and heathen race. The fact that the official literature of the time is littered with references to the Indians only as "Coolies", confirmed this high-handed attitude, one lacking in basic human decency, as pointed out by Jane Swinton. Indeed this was reflected in the fact that after all was said and done, throughout the 108 days of the voyage the Indian emigrants had experienced untold anguish, despair, suffering and ultimately death, yet as far as the records are concerned, they remain voiceless; a mute statistic in both the Captain's *Journal* and the inquiry that followed. The echo of this loud silence leaves a void of speculation. But the fact remains that the selective use of the Indian Interpreters, who were well-versed in the emigrant's languages, has left much to be desired.

Nevertheless the insights gained from the *Journal* opens a window through which we could view with greater clarity, and thus apply better judgement to a relatively unknown aspect of the East Indian indentured emigration experience - the epic voyage of an uncommon quest, deeply ingrained in the very being of a remarkably tenacious people. Whether or not "push" or "pull" factors took precedence (more than likely it was a mixture of both!), it cannot be assumed that the emigrants on the*Salsette* were, in toto, a *tabula rasa.* On the contrary, many among them were, as individuals, highly sensitive to the implications of their actions. So that, for 124 of them, the hope and dream of crossing the dreaded and (for the high castes) tabooed "Kala pani" (dark water) for a better life, was a risk worth taking. They had, indeed, gambled everything and lost.

For those who were fortunate enough to land barely alive and profoundly shaken, the hard struggle that would, in the years to come, become their essential experience on the plantations was only momentarily obscured by the more immediate concern of preserving life and limb. And to compound their problems, the fragile-looking, though dignified Indians were not welcomed with open arms by the local Creole society, who viewed them with intense hostility.

Having left the confines and dangers of the ship, who knows what relief and mixture of emotions they may have felt as they made their way for the first time in over three months, on the firm ground of the lush island which, until now, they only knew by name, as "Chinedad", to the various sugar estates where they were to be bound as replacement labour. And so, in the process of repeopling the Caribbean, 366 years after Columbus thought he had reached India, the indentured Indians had come voluntarily via a tortuous and tragic passage (a transforming experience which brought them together as *jahaji bhai* - the brotherhood of the ship), to occupy, especially in these early years, the renovated, but still cramped, unsatisfactory barrack dwellings and labour on the same land, vacated by the African slaves, who had themselves survived the horrors of their "Middle Passage".

In the aftermath of the *Salsette's* voyage, Captain Swinton's call for an inquiry and his wife's safe-keeping and publication of his *Journal* led, in subsequent years, to improvements in the facilities available on the "Coolie" emigrant ships, including a hospital on deck, a nurse, purified water, improved diet and more Indian assistants. The overall effect was a marked decline in the number of deaths on the Indian emigrants' long and unforgettable journey, the *other* middle passage, which would, with each day, remain ever present in their collective memory, even though they would gradually be released (at times, painfully), from their ancient Indian roots and become increasingly anchored to their modern Caribbean moorings.

Ron Ramdin
London
April 1994

Appendix 1

Mortality upon voyages from Calcutta to the Westindies, 1850/1 to 1860/1

	% females to males	% children to adults	Mortality
1850/1	9	5	3.6
1851/2	17	11	4.5
1852/3	24	17	5.6
1853/4	14	8	3.3
1854/5	18	7	2.8
1855/6	36	11	5.8
1856/7	35	15	17.3
1857/8	66	29	13.2
1858/9	---	---	9.8
1859/60	---	---	12.0
1860/1	---	---	8.5

Sources: Sir Clinton Murdoch to Herman Merivale, Colonial Office, 11 August 1858; Report by Emigration Commissioners, return of emigration to the Westindies, 1861/2.

Appendix 2

Mortality on ships to the Westindies, 1856/7

	Passengers				No. of deaths	Mortality as % of total
	Men	Women	Children	Total		
Wellesley	254	84	44	382	22	5.75
Bucephalus	252	84	44	380	45	11.84
Sir Robert Seppings	197	59	35	291	61	20.96
Roman Emperor	207	68	38	313	88	28.11
Adelaide	213	62	29	304	25	8.22
Sir George Seymour	238	75	41	354	36	10.17
Eveline	231	96	60	387	72	24.53
Maidstone	268	68	39	375	92	24.53
Merchantman	239	96	50	385	120	31.17
Granville	154	100	55	309	37	11.97
Burmah	230	58	38	326	49	15.03
Scindian	156	81	51	288	60	20.83
Total	2,639	1,931	524	4,094	707	17.27

Above tables courtesy of Hugh Tinker - *A New System of Slavery* (Hansib Publishing)

Appendix 3

List of Sandbach Tinne's "coolie ships".

Built	Name	Tons	Length	Breadth	Depth	Builder	Remarks
1828	*Sandbach*	435	---	---	---	At Liverpool	Broken up 1878
1829	*Demerara*	214	---	---	---	At Dumbarton	Sold to Dublin
1832	*Johnstone*	436	---	---	---	At Liverpool	
1836	*Leonora*	345	---	---	---		
1861	*George Rainy*	519	137.3	28.9	19.1	Clark, Liverpool	
1863	*Hesper*	309	124	26.8	13.1	New Brunswick	Became hulk W. Africa
1864	*Zemindar*	1096	191	35.4	22.6	Holderness, Liverpool	
1864	*Pandora*	1156	213.7	35	21.6	Connell	
1865	*Fairlie*	599	148	29.1	18.8	Hedderwick, Glasgow	
1865	*Kiltearn*	599	147.7	29	18.7	Hedderwick, Glasgow	
1867	*Rona*	638	156.4	29.6	18.6	Stephen	
1868	*Saint Kilda*	865	188.6	32.7	19	Stephen	
1870	*Ailsa*	1112	213.1	35.2	19.8	Connell	
1871	*Mora ex Lothair*	643	160	31.1	18.6	Blumer	
1875	*Jura*	1285	230.3	37.1	20.8	Connell	
1877	*Shiela*	1295	228.7	36.8	21	Connell	
1877	*Brenda*	1281	228	36.8	21.1	Connell	
1865	*British Nation*	1302	216.2	35.3	22.9	Walpole, Dublin	
1867	*British Statesman*	1262	217	36	22	Royden, Liverpool	Lost off Hughli, 1885
1881	*Columba*	1794	263	39.1	24.1	Potter	
1882	*Orealla*	1843	250.5	40.2	24	Royden	
1882	*Godiva*	2054	269	41.6	24.3	Royden	
1882	*Stronsa*	2053	269	41.6	24.3	Royden	
1882	*Genista*	1852	270.5	39.2	24	Potter	

Appendix 4

List of James Nourse's Fleet.

Built	Name	Tons	Length	Br'dth	Depth	Builder	Remarks
1854	*Jorawur*	1736	235	41.5	26.4	Mare, London	
1858	*Adamant*	815	174.2	30	19.2	At Hull	
1861	*Ganges I*	839	192	33.2	20.6	Pile, Sunderland	
1867	*Jumna*	1048	208.6	34.1	20.1	Pile, Sunderland	
1868	*Syria*	1010	207.7	34.1	20.8	Pile, Sunderland	
1869	*Neva*	1109	214.4	34.9	21.1	Lawrie, Glasgow	
1869	*Stockbridge*	1495	230.4	38.7	24.7	Oswald, Sunderland	
1868	*Grecian*	1272	223.9	36.2	22.5	Scott, Greenock	Bought in 1870s
1874	*Foyle*	1664	243	38.8	24.2	Oswald, Sunderland	
1875	*Bann*	1667	250.1	38.9	24.2	Oswald, Sunderland	
1876	*Liffey*	1402	226.1	37.1	22.3	Oswald, Southampton	
1877	*Boyne*	1415	226.1	37.1	22.3	Oswald, Southampton	
1878	*Lee*	1485	240.4	37.1	22.4	Oswald, Southampton	
1874	*Allanshaw*	1589	262.8	40.2	23	Simons, Renfrew	Bought about 1880
1866	*The Bruce*	1200	224.2	35.6	22.3	Mansell, Glasgow	Bought about 1880
1869	*Hereford*	1469	241.1	37.2	23.2	Elder, Glasgow	Bought about 1881/2
1882	*Ganges II*	1529	241	37.2	22.5	Osbourne, Sunderland	
1865	*British Peter*	1428	247.5	36.4	22.5	Harland & Wolff	Bought 1883
1884	*Main*	1691	256.4	38.3	23.1	Russell	
1885	*Moy*	1697	257.6	38.3	23.2	Russell	
1885	*Avoca*	1703	257.5	38.2	23.2	Russell	
1886	*Erne*	1692	255.6	38.3	23.2	Russell	
1886	*Rhine*	1691	257.2	38.3	23.1	Russell	
1887	*Elbe*	1693	257	38.2	23.1	Russell	
1887	*Volga I*	1698	257.5	38.2	23.2	Russell	
1875	*Rhone ex Gilroy*	1768	259.2	39.9	23.2	Elder, Glasgow	Bought about 1890
1884	*Avon ex Dunnolly*	1572	255.6	37.6	22.6	Connell	Bought about 1890
1891	*Volga II*	1817	270.7	39	22.5	Connell	
1893	*Arno*	1825	270.7	39	22.5	Connell	
1893	*Ems*	1829	270.7	39	22.5	Connell	
1894	*Mersey*	1820	270.7	39	22.5	Connell	
1894	*Forth*	1820	270.7	39	22.5	Connell	
1894	*Clyde*	1840	270.9	39	22.5	Russell	
1875	*Lena ex Baron Colonsay*	1733	269	40.1	23.5	J. E. Scott	Bought from Baine & Johnston, 1894

JOURNAL OF A VOYAGE

WITH

COOLIE EMIGRANTS,

FROM

CALCUTTA TO TRINIDAD.

BY

CAPTAIN AND MRS. SWINTON,

LATE OF THE SHIP "SALSETTE."

EDITED BY JAMES CARLILE, D.D., L.L.D.,

MINISTER OF SALEM CHAPEL, WOOLWICH.

LONDON:

ALFRED W. BENNETT, BISHOPSGATE STREET,

AND ALL BOOKSELLERS.

Price Sixpence.

A liberal allowance for gratuitous circulation—apply to the Editor. The profits (if any) devoted to a benevolent object.

TO

THE SOCIETY OF FRIENDS,

WITH WHOM I HAVE BEEN ASSOCIATED,

DURING THE WHOLE OF MY PUBLIC LIFE, IN THE CAUSE OF

NEGRO EMANCIPATION;

AND WHOM I HAVE ALWAYS FOUND THE TRUE AND TRUSTY FRIENDS OF

FREEDOM AND OF MAN,

I Respectfully Dedicate

THESE PAGES.

JAMES CARLILE.

WOOLWICH, *February* 22, 1859

JOURNAL OF A VOYAGE

WITH

COOLIE EMIGRANTS.

THE British ship *Salsette* was chartered in Calcutta, to convey a cargo of Coolie emigrants from that city to our island of Trinidad. She sailed from the Hooghly on the 17th day of March last; was under the command of an experienced seaman, Captain Swinton; had an adequate body of competent sailors; met with no disaster from storm or hurricane; and arrived at her destination early in July. She embarked Coolies to the number of 324, infants included, being equal to 274 adults; and during the voyage she lost, by death, 120 Coolies! It will be remembered that there was no prevalent epidemic to account for this excessive mortality. Individual cases of cholera and of fever there were; but these cases were all isolated ones, and no kind of epidemic assailed the Coolies.

How shall we account for such mortality—an average of more than one per day during the entire passage? Was the Captain a thoughtless, bold, dashing sailor, reckless of human life? He was the very opposite—kind, generous, and humane. The luxuries of his chief cabin, the delicacies provided for his wife's comfort, were dispensed with a liberal hand to men, women, and children, when their state of health required them. His excellent wife, too, was on board; and by her constant and kindly attention soothed the sorrows, and mitigated the sufferings of many a dying Coolie. Indeed, on board that ship, she was like another Florence Nightingale in the hospital at Scutari; and but for the attendance and care of this angel of mercy, humanly speaking, the mortality, large as it was, would have been much larger.

But, even apart from the known humanity and kindness of the captain and his wife, there was another reason—always potent and influential with human nature—which would lead us to expect unremitting attention to the health of the Coolies. The pecuniary interests of the ship's owners were at stake.

4

Every death that took place among the Coolies was to them a loss of £13; so that by the deaths that did take place they lost about £1500 of their charter money. That Captain Swinton was aware of this the following note, from his agent at Calcutta, will prove:—

"MY DEAR CAPTAIN SWINTON,—Government will only pay you on so many Coolies landed alive. The *Roman Emperor* lost 86 out of 288 taken on board here, consequently lost £1000 —not one man died this side of the Cape. Another ship lost a larger sum; so be cautious.—Yours truly,

"JOHN WREINHOLT.

"24th February, 1858."

But that the mortality was not caused by any want of attention to the Coolies, is proved to demonstration by the following medical testimony. Captain Swinton, on arriving at the island, requested an official investigation of the causes of the heavy mortality. This was granted, and resulted in the placing in his hands the following decisive testimony:—

"Trinidad, 23rd July, 1858.

"I certify that, notwithstanding the heavy mortality which occurred on board the ship *Salsette*, among the Indian immigrant passengers, I believe that the said immigrants were carefully attended to, both by Captain Swinton and his officers. I believe, further, that the mortality depended on causes beyond their control. "HENRY MITCHELL, M.D.,

"Agent-General of Emigration.

"To Captain E. Swinton,
"Ship *Salsette*."

The sequel is sad: Captain Swinton, on his homeward voyage, called at New York through stress of weather. He urged his wife to return by a mail steamer, and gave her, among other documents, the journal he had daily written during his voyage. In a few days after leaving, his fine ship foundered, carrying her gallant captain and a large crew to the bottom of the Atlantic. His widow has, with fidelity, copied the following extract from the journal of her husband. We certify the accuracy of the copy.

EXTRACTS FROM THE DIARY OF CAPTAIN SWINTON,

ON HIS PASSAGE FROM CALCUTTA TO TRINIDAD.

March 17*th*, 1858. Left Calcutta for Trinidad; several Coolies sick.

18*th*.- An old woman died of cholera; she was rejected on coming on board, but eighteen men would not come without her.

19*th*. Several Coolies sick.

21*st*. A little girl, six years of age, died of dysentery in its mother's arms.

24*th*. An old woman died of diarrhœa.

26*th*. A little orphan girl, four years of age, died in a state of great emaciation; she was in this state when put on board, with an aunt, only ten years old, to take care of her. An old woman brought a baby, two years old, quite dead from starvation, having taken no food, and having lost its father and mother before embarkation. Sent for the little girl two years old, before mentioned, and from her history it appears that her brother and sister died at the "depôt" before embarkation, and the infant was sent with her. Three children, from six to ten years old, were sent on board without parents. Saw a little boy dying on deck; a most dreadfully emaciated creature; won't eat.

26*th*. A little boy died, to whom my attention was called yesterday. An infant found dead below; its mother was sick and unable to nourish it. Preserved milk much needed; sad howling of infants who were dying for want of milk.

27*th*. About twenty sick. Died, of dysentery, one infant boy five years, and a young man twenty-eight years old. An old man and his sons were called on deck and asked if they had not been rejected by the doctor, when they replied they had; but the Sircar told them if they did not go he would beat them out of the depôt. This is the second instance of such an occurrence.

28*th*. Two women, who had been ill some days, died. One Coolie died from fear, seeing so many die. A young woman died of cholera, after three days' illness. Fed several children and old men with chickens, rice, and sago (not allowed by the ship). It appears they are sinking for want of food suited to them. Dried fish for adults, and milk for children wanted.

29th. One infant dead; but Topaz cannot interpret for doctor. A little girl died, and on inquiry no one knows her; she had a sister aged fourteen. Jane (Mrs. Swinton) feeding the sick with sago; one woman eating it who is dying. Jane and myself giving mutton broth to the sick and feeble (not allowed by the ship).

30th. One woman died. Went below and found a little boy (whose mother had died some days since) dead, from want. Jane giving arrowroot to sick children, orphans, women, and men.

31st. A man found dead, aged seventy-five, after lingering since we left the Sund Head, though all that was possible was done for him by warm bath and so forth, but he refused all food of late. A Coolie woman cut her own head going to jump overboard. Two died—an old man, who was rejected at the depôt, and a girl ten years old, who has refused food for four days against all persuasion.

April 2nd. A Coolie, twenty-one years old, died; his illness known to the doctor only two days. A little boy got a bath, whose mother died a few days since; but the lazy Topaz neglected to bring him to the doctor.

3rd. An infant died who lost its mother. A Coolie fell and cut his eye.

4th. An infant died, and a girl twelve years old; also a fine lad, sixteen, gasping. Another girl died, ten years old. Two children died, three years old, and a little girl, aged seven years, who lost her parents on board, and has been lingering ten days.

7th. A little girl, five years old, died with marks on the throat and back, and foot bruised (supposed murdered). Flogged father and mother; the father known to be of a desperately bad character in his own country. An old woman, fifty years old, died; the doctor said she had been rejected. Was allowed to come because many others would not come without her.

8th. A girl, three years old, died.

9th. Boy, fifteen, died; this completes the family of father and two sons, rejected at depôt for spleen enlargement.

10th. A little blind girl died, and now its mother is all but gone.

7

11th and *12th*. Several sick.

13th. An old man died from debility. Another old man and two women very bad. Two men died of old age, diarrhœa, and debility.

15th. Another man died. Twenty-eight adults now dead.

16th. One old woman died, and four sick Coolies, all merry to-day.

17th. A little girl, three years old, died, and Jane's protegée nearly done up also. Jane's protegée died, aged four, after very great pains to keep her up; but it fretted after its mother.

18th. A little girl, two years old, died, though no previous illness; it lost its mother about ten days since, and its father appears sorry for it. A girl, about fourteen, sick, who was sent by the depôt Sircar, with an infant, two years old, whose mother died at the depôt.

19th. A young man of twenty died, who was only brought to the doctor yesterday. A little girl died from inability of its mother to suckle it. A boy, six years old, dying; this is the first time he has been brought to the doctor, though he is nearly dead now, and cannot last long. A young woman fell down the fore hatch and hurt her spine very much; doctor put leeches to it, but would have known nothing of the accident but for the mate seeing her fall.

20th. One child and an old woman died.

21st. An infant died from want of proper nourishment, as biscuits and rice would not keep it alive without milk.

22nd. One man, aged thirty-five, died.

23rd. A child, three years old, died from neglect by the mother.

24th. Fine boy, fourteen years old, taken suddenly with cholera, and was brought on deck very weak; the doctor prescribed for him.

25th. A woman died and an infant, and I fear there will soon be two more gone.

26th. One woman died through fear, after having been chastised for giving her child a poisonous nut. These people pine after being put on board, being in doubt as to their destination. A little child, so much neglected by its mother, is dying.

27th. A fine little baby has died.

28th. The doctor had several children put into hot baths.

29th. The sick all better. Got the launch boat cleared to

8

convert it into an hospital for the sick; the smell below being so dreadful, though everything done to prevent it. I regret it was not done on leaving Calcutta, as I believe many would have been saved, the sickness arising entirely from bad smells. Each time I go below the smell makes me sick. I truly pity, but the cold weather likely to come on deterred me from turning the boat into an hospital; but the doctor thinks it the lesser evil of the two, therefore got it thoroughly cleansed and purified, by lime, for six adults.

30*th.* A child died.

May 3*rd.* A woman died of dysentery. This makes seventy dead. It is dreadful mortality; still any one who had ever sailed with them would not wonder at it, as they are so badly selected at the depôt, and so many diseased sent on board. Besides, their habits are so beastly, and personal cleanliness so neglected, and being such a weakly emaciated set, they require a suitable number of male and female nurses, who should be adequately remunerated, to look after and attend to them.

4*th.* A little boy, who eats ravenously, has very enlarged spleen, losing flesh, and very cross.

9*th.* Coolies complain that twelve ounces of rice, without dholl, is not enough, therefore give them two ounces more rice as an equivalent.

11*th.* Boy of ten died; the last of the rejected of the splenetic family.

12*th.* One twin child died.

13*th.* Doctor found several sick not reported.

14*th.* One Coolie died.

15*th.* A Coolie died, forty-five years of age.

16*th.* Jane feeding the sick with mutton broth. Boy of fifteen died to-day, who would not come for prescription before yesterday morning. Doctor suggests the propriety of not giving any more of these people medicine, they having such an objection and aversion to it that they will rather pine and die than apply for it in time; but as we had no country medicine (*i. e.*, herbs), which their faith lies in, I think it is well to continue now.

17*th.* An old woman died from sheer debility; rejected at the depôt. I intend applying to the Government at home on behalf of my owners, for having had such people put on board; the captain having no control in the matter. A nice little girl, five years old, died, who got a relapse of diarrhœa, although at one time she was quite lively. This makes about fifty adults.

9

19th. A boy, twelve years, and a girl, seven years old, died.

20th. A little girl died. Jane getting music up to amuse the Coolies.

21st. A little orphan girl, five years old, died, after lingering long, the last of her family; in fact, they appear to die in families.

23rd. A woman and man died.

24th. A woman died, the mother of the twin babies, of which one is left to the father.

25th. The mother of the yellow woman who died some days since, died to-day. Sick personally attended by Jane, and supplied with soups, etc., from the cuddy table; cungie or sago every morning, and the children also, three times a-day. Still everything is unavailable.

26th. Three Coolies died; a man, a fine girl, eighteen, who attended a little orphan boy, and a boy, twelve, who had cholera some time since and got better, but relapsed. An old woman died, who would not confess that she was ill, and only came before the doctor a few hours before her death. This mortality is dreadful, and without any means of being checked. A great reformation is required in the system of Cooley emigration. One of the twins all but gone.

27th. A woman very bad with diarrhœa; when given medicine to check it, gave way to great passion, and knocked her head against the deck. Still getting soup from the cabin.

28th. The doctor says he wants medicine (chalk-mixture), and two men died of diarrhœa. Coolie blind man dead; a little girl and its mother almost gone also. Doctor asked me if I intended to call at St. Helena, as he was out of chalk-powder and laudanum, both essentially required for the Coolies' complaint. I replied, Not unless he insisted on it, as it would put the ship to considerable expense by doing so.

June 1st. One child died of dropsy. The doctor and Jane attending the sick. Doctor wrote me a note, begging me to call at St. Helena for medicine, which I must now do, in compliance with the terms of the charter-party. Woman died.

3rd. Hove to off James Town, St. Helena.

5th. One man died of dysentery; the doctor dissected him, and found diseased tubes: Jane gave up her cabin to have him dissected. One boy, fifteen, and one girl, eight, died, and several sick.

6th. Sick Coolie getting beef soup. Doctor found a man, who was suspected of foul play to his child, very weak. Cross-questioned two interpreters and our third-mate, who had sailed with Coolies before, respecting Coolies' ships, and took notes. From all I can learn, they are infinitely better treated and cared for here than in any other ships, and mortality not greater. Interpreter says 105 have died here, and he is not far off the truth; I asked this question to see how far I could rely on his information.

7th. Infant died; and many sick found who are afraid to take our medicine. Doctor going over his list to see if his book and accounts agreed. And many vexations from these people, arising from their dirty and lying habits; and make 110, all told, or about 80 adults deceased to date. Fearful!

8th. One man died, age thirty-five. Another man died; this is the last of another family, who said this morning he was much better, and really appeared far from a dying man; but it is most odd, how very suddenly these people go off from apparent medium health to general debility, though kept up with port wine and soup; and were it not for the unremitting attention of Jane, many of them would have sunk under the disease. I hope she may not herself fall a prey to her disinterested kindness, but she seems to have no fear.

10th. A man dying, aged twenty-five, of debility and dysentery, after long lingering. Sick Coolies getting soup from cabin table.

11th. Another woman died, aged thirty, who denied being sick, until her weakly state betrayed her, a couple of days since, and even then she declared she was not ill.

12th. A Coolie, the seventh objected to, died after lingering a long time, and is the last of her family of two children, husband, and self. Had serious conversation with the doctor about such weakly people being put on board the ship.

18th. One woman died who hurt her spine. Several fresh cases of concealment of diarrhœa.

19th. A woman dying of diarrhœa. Another death from diarrhœa, and several won't confess their illness till too far gone, which shows the necessity of having nurses to look after them.

21st. The Coolies very musical.

22nd. Coolies performing.

23rd. Coolies having some native games and war-dances.

25th. Little girl, two years old, died of diarrhœa, and neglected by its mother. Coolies performing.

26th. One woman, twenty-five, and several others, nearly dead, and all this within a few days.

11

27th. One woman died, aged twenty-five. One man died after long sickness; had swelled legs, an almost infallible sign of dissolution amongst these people. Doctor thinks if they had got two or three doses of castor-oil on leaving, and more exercise, it would have saved many of them. Coolies performing on deck.

28th. One man, twenty-five years old, died after fourteen days' diarrhœa, but only complained the last three days; several others I fear will go. The late damp weather had something, I think, to do with it.

29th. An old man died, fifty years of age, of dysentery and bleeding at the mouth. Several others nearly gone. Purpose (D.V.) to muster Coolies to-morrow, but fear it will be a bad one.

30th. Mustered the Coolies, and find only 108 men, 61 women, and 30 children under ten years of age, 2 infants, and 2 interpreters, left, of the 323 or 324 we sailed from Calcutta with, and 3, I fear, will die before we can get them landed.

July 2nd.—A girl of fifteen died. Dr. Anderson, and custom-house officer and harbour-master, came on board; thought the Coolies a miserable set, and the mortality dreadful, and were surprised at such people being sent. They expressed themselves well pleased with the ventilation and accommodation.

3rd. A little girl, three years old, died. Dr. Mitchell inspected all, and mustered orphans—six of whom are under ten years, and are to be sent to an orphan asylum; the other sixteen above ten years old, doubtful. He expressed his ideas of disapprobation of the Calcutta emigration management; got the ten sick sent away to hospital. Dr. Mercer, of the hospital, and Mr. Cottins, chief-clerk of the government office, came on board; talked to the doctor about the people sent to hospital.

5th. Two sick men sent on shore.

6th. Went on shore with five children, orphans; twenty Coolies left on board, and the two interpreters. Saw Dr. Mitchell, and found only 182 adults landed alive. Had an interview with Dr. Mitchell, the emigration agent, about the injustice to this ship to suffer through the omission of the doctor not making any proviso to be paid for any objectionable people. Seven out of nine who died were allowed to ship *Cambria.*

7th. In consequence of the great mortality, I requested that an investigation might be held, which was granted.

21st. Got notice to take mate to government house, and go before emigration committee, about treatment. At

12

2 p.m. met. After examining us and the doctor, decided the Coolies were not in a fit state to ship, but would not allow for the seven objectionable ones.

REMARKS BY MRS. SWINTON.

I must preface the following observations by stating that the captain of a ship about to carry Coolies to the West Indies has no voice whatever, either in their selection, or in the choice of the doctor, or in anything connected with their emigration. His sole duty is to navigate the ship according to the rules laid down by the charter-party. My opinion is, in justice to the ship-owners, that the captain ought to be allowed to nominate a doctor on behalf of the owners, to make the selection of the Coolies in conjunction with the doctor appointed to the ship, and that sufficient time be given to the doctors to make the proper inspection. One day only was given to the doctor who accompanied us in charge of the Coolies. Again, I think the doctor in charge of the Coolies should be one who can speak their language fluently, instead of being wholly dependent on an interpreter, who may understand English very indifferently; as, from their station, they are necessarily of that class. The manner in which the Coolies are collected together in Calcutta is from native travellers being sent out into the country and villages, to induce them to emigrate by fine promises. These travellers bring in the scum of the villages as well as some desirable emigrants. They should be kept at least a month at the depôt, to get them into a fit state to bear a three months' voyage. The head man of the depôt, called Sircar, is a native; and is either not sufficiently paid to perform his duties conscientiously, or is what I believe few of the natives are, trustworthy. The Sircar, whether native or otherwise, should be a person of strict integrity; and the situation ought to demand a gentleman of that class, and not be left to subordinates. *Vide* the diary of Captain Swinton, out of the 324 Coolies who came on board, I do not believe five, at most, either know where they are going, or what is to be their occupation. My heart often yearned over them, in thinking of the way they were entrapped, as many of them asked me to recommend them to get a good situation on their arrival at the island. A great many on board were not calculated for the labour they would have to perform. With respect to food and

13

clothing, dry biscuit with water for breakfast, is not suitable food for a woman nursing, as bread is considered most injurious for all emigrants, as being the main cause of bringing on dysentery. I think to allow them more rice, with some fish, would be better. We had no dried fish on board; they do not like sago, which was amply supplied. I consider fowls would be very desirable for weakly women—they being very cheap in India—as they often craved them from me; and I believe, had they been given such things, many lives would have been saved. Preserved milk is most requisite for women and children; we had none put on board by the Government, but what little I had I shared with them. They only get two meals a-day, but I think if the same quantity were given in three meals it would be better, as they eat too much at the second. Some hide what they cannot eat, and before they eat it, it turns sour, and brings on diarrhœa; though every means were used to prevent their hiding any away. The number and class of interpreters should be changed: they are not paid for, though the ship is obliged to carry them, and has not even a voice in their selection. They ought to be quick, intelligent, and trustworthy; and *two*, the number we had, were not sufficient. The doctor was often in a dilemma, when the most intelligent of the two was sick; and had he died, the doctor not speaking the language, the sick would have been in a bad way. I strongly recommend that every ship carrying Coolies should have a native apothecary in addition to their doctor, and that the ship be supplied with the herbs used by the natives in sickness, as it is next to an impossibility to get them to take our medicine. I would recommend that *tank* water be substituted for *Hooghly* water, which, though passed through a sort of filter, retains much that is unfit for use. The clothes supplied are both badly selected and insufficient for the voyage. A couple of extra bales of clothes would add much to their comfort, so that the doctor might be able to give some to those that required them. The Coolies themselves should not have the charge of their clothes, on account of their dirty habits; indeed, some of them would have arrived in a state of nudity, had I not supplied them from my own wardrobe.

Female nurses, well selected, are absolutely necessary, not only to attend the sick, but to attend those remedies ordered by the doctor, and which, even in their apparently demoralized state, they will not allow a man to give them; but which in many cases might have saved their lives, as was the case with the men who had got lavement from the interpreters. The female Coolies not having that sympathy for each other which we have, I think it highly improper to plunge the females into cold water every day, there being times when such is very injurious; one woman, I am afraid, died from the effects of this cold water plunging. One day, when ordered by the doctor for all to run round for exercise, one woman *enciente* did not like to go, but was ashamed to tell the doctor why, and came and told me to tell him; by having proper female nurses these difficulties would be obviated. We found exercise, such as their native dances, very useful in keeping up a good state of health—an experiment which we tried. Music is also very desirable, and keeping them employed in any way, to prevent them from thinking and drooping. They have no morality whatever: if they fancy each other, they become man and wife for the time being, and change again when they please. The parents of girls will sell their children for a few rupees. I may here mention that in the island, on the plantations which I visited, I found the same immorality was carried on, and no provision for instructing them in Christianity; on the contrary, their own heathen processions were allowed to be carried on, but good care was taken of their bodies, as there was a doctor to take charge of them. I was much gratified at the orphan-school which I visited, both as to the cleanliness of the school and the orphans (some brought by our ship) and their training. I think day-schools, for the children whose parents are at work, are much wanted, as they might be by that means instructed in Christianity.

To give an idea of their views, one day, in talking to some of the Coolies of the Supreme Being, they said, "Your beef and mutton very good God." These people being very subservient and tractable, I believe there would be less difficulty in bringing them to embrace Christianity than any other race of people I have met. As an example, I could point to a previous voyage where I had 500 Chinamen on board for four months, and they seemed to be a most determined and self-willed people, who thought a great deal of their joss, and were quite opposed to the others in character. As an example of the simplicity of the Coolie character, a father wanted to marry his daughter against her will to a man, for a few rupees, and she came and told me her tale, the tears in her eyes, when I called the young man she liked, and married her to him, they lived happily, and left the ship believing themselves properly married, and, feeling inte-

15

rested in them, I visited the plantation they were on, and found them quite happy. I asked them if they liked their new employment. They said they preferred Calcutta. I said, "You will earn plenty of money to go back," when they replied, all they earned went into their stomachs. The doctor and self gave them some money on leaving.

They improved in health soon after being on the island. Many of them cried bitterly on leaving the ship, saying they would have no mam-sab where they were going, *i. e.*, myself. They made the best appearance they could when the planters came to select them. (It looks very like slavery.) They were put into boats in sixes and sevens like cattle, and sent to their different destinations. I pitied them much at parting with them. I had been the first captain's wife who arrived at Trinidad with Coolies; and, from the great mortality we had, the people seemed to shun me like a mad dog on my arrival, and consequently I received no hospitality from the inhabitants, though much thanked by the emigration agent, who seemed much surprised at my venturing with such people; but a desire to see the habits of these people induced me to remain on board, though my friends in Calcutta tried to prevail on me to remain till the ship returned.

I strongly recommend that in every Coolie ship there should be a hospital on deck, for the desirability of which *vide* the notes in Captain Swinton's Diary on the subject. I think it would be decidedly beneficial to appoint nightly watches to attend to the cleanliness, and to wait on the sick. The doctor and Captain Swinton had such, and personally superintended it every two hours. This is not a captain's duty; he did it through humanity and in the interest of his owners. Without self-adulation, but for the benefit of others, I must say, that, were it not for the unremitting attention of Captain Swinton and myself, the mortality would have been considerably augmented. I think it is most unjust and illiberal to the owners of any Coolie-ship to be paid only for such as are landed alive, particularly when put on board in such a diseased state by the emigration office in Calcutta. Why have one law for our Indian emigrants to the West India colonies, and another for our English emigrants to Australia? Had my husband been spared to land in England, it was his intention to lay it all before the Government, the injustice practised towards Coolie-ships calling for such a measure.

16

I hope that the few remarks which I have penned may, with the assistance of God, tend towards promoting the welfare of this unfortunate race of people, and may be the means of interesting some kind and philanthropic persons on their behalf. My heart sickens when I think of their sufferings; so I must conclude.

JANE SWINTON.

Having passed a year in China, I think this a favourable opportunity of calling the attention of the "slaves'" friend to the system of Coolie emigration from China. The Coolies there are entrapped into a depôt kept at Macao until a ship can be chartered, when they are placed on board, not knowing any particulars respecting their destination, etc., and which has been the cause of some of our captains and crews having been murdered. During my stay at Hong-Kong, two ships came in with Chinese Coolies in a state of mutiny, and, when brought before the magistrates, gave as a reason for their conduct, that they were put on board without having any knowledge of where they were to be taken to. I believe sentence of death was passed on them, but commuted to imprisonment for life. Our ship was offered a large sum to take Chinese Coolies, but has declined; and we took Chinese emigrants to Australia, 500 in number, of whom only eight died after three months and a day passage. Proper accommodation is not provided for the Chinese Coolies. They are (to use the phrase known in slave-ships) "packed and sold," and merely "paddy" (unclean rice) and oil put on board for their food.

Printed by W. J. Johnson, 121, Fleet Street, London, E.C.

Other titles in the Hansib *Coolie Odyssey* series

A New System of Slavery: The Export of Indian Labour Overseas 1830-1920 *by Hugh Tinker*. The first comprehensive historical survey of the, at the time little known, migration of Indian labour overseas to supply the plantations of the Caribbean. *Paperback £11.99*

India in the Caribbean *edited by Dr David Dabydeen and Dr Brinsley Samaroo.* A collection of essays, poems and prose by leading Indo-Caribbean scholars and writers, on East Indian history and culture in the Caribbean. *Paperback £8.95. Hardback £11.95*

Benevolent Neutrality: Indian Government Policy and Labour Migration to British Guiana 1854-1884 *by Dr Basdeo Mangru.* A detailed, scholarly essay on Indian migration, which studies the background of the indentured labourers and explains the economic, political and cultural factors which encouraged migration. *Hardback £12.95*

Coolie Odyssey *by David Dabydeen.* Dabydeen's second collection of poetry probing the experience of diaspora, the journeying from India to the Caribbean then to Britain. *Paperback £3.95*

Inseparable Humanity *by Shridath S. Ramphal.* An anthology of reflections by the former Commonwealth Secretary-General. *Hardback £14.95*

Forbidden Freedom - The Story of British Guiana *by Dr. Cheddi Jagan.* A classic document of anti-colonist and anti-imperialist struggle from one of the veteran leaders of the Third World. *Paperback £6.00*

King of the Carnival and Other Stories *by Willi Chen.* A unique collection of short stories from the Caribbean, capturing the violence, trickery, pathos and racial comedy of Trinidadian society. *Paperback £5.95*

Passion and Exile *by Frank Birbalsingh.* A wide ranging collection of essays that offer an illuminating commentary on the literary and social history of the English speaking Caribbean. *Paperback £7.95*

The Open Prison. *A novel by Angus Richmond.* The author, an Indo-Guyanese writer won the Casa de las Americas Award in 1978 for his first novel A Kind of

Loving. The Open Prison tells the story of Angela, a mulatto growing up in British Guiana prior to the First World War, slowly awakened to the turmoils of a volatile society. *Paperback £4.95*

The Web of Tradition - Uses of Allusion in V.S. Naipaul's Fiction *by Dr. John Thieme.* An exciting study of the work of one of the Caribbean's major and most controversial novelists. *Paperback £6.95*

Indo-Westindian Cricket *by Prof. Frank Birbalsingh and Clem Shiwcharan.* Two brilliant essays on Westindian cricket by two of the region's leading cultural historians highlighting the genius of cricketers like Kanhai, Kallicharan and Ramadhin. *Hardback £7.95*